PRAISE F[ ]
What It Means t[ ]

Being a man in contemporary culture can be extremely confusing. Rhett Smith brings light to the subject in *What It Means to Be a Man*. I highly recommend it.

Gary Chapman, author of *The 5 Love Languages*

What It Means to Be a Man is my favorite kind of book, the kind that sets you on a journey of self-discovery. This book is a bridge between the man you are and the man you're becoming — read it.

Scott McClellan, author of *Tell Me a Story*

This book moves beyond the rah-rah Braveheart masculinity. Rhett Smith is aware of the deadly symptoms that plague men from being "men," but wisely directs men toward core issues beyond adrenaline-based masculinity. This book is accessible for readers and non-readers alike and also brings the ideas down to earth through practical application in each chapter. I know plenty of boys who need to become men, and this book will help.

Sean McGever, area director at YoungLife

Understanding the "fix it now" attitude with which most of us men attack life, Rhett meets every man right in this place by succinctly capturing the core pain we feel inside. Then he just as succinctly offers us real tangible "fixable" challenges for change. As a man, I like that. This book reads like a "cookbook" for how we as men can recognize, call out in ourselves, and do something about (i.e., fix) the obstacles that hold us back from living out of the truest calling as husbands, fathers, brothers, sons, bosses, and friends.

Todd Sandel, LMFT, executive director of LifeGate Counseling Center in Atlanta, Georgia

In this simple, honest book, Rhett Smith paints a gracious portrait of masculinity and how it relates to the spiritual life. The conversations that result from his stories and wisdom are exactly the ones we need to be having.

Jason Boyett, author of *O Me of Little Faith* and *A Guy's Guide to Life*

Sometimes you read a book and think the person really had two chapters of good material and spread it over eleven chapters. In this case, Rhett doesn't waste the reader's time or energy. Short chapters, easy to read, relevant material, and straight-to-the-point reflection questions make for fruitful reading and meaningful onramps for group discussion time.

Keenan Barber, pastor of youth and young adults at Bel Air Presbyterian Church in Los Angeles

Simple and to-the-point, *What It Means to Be a Man* is a practical conversation starter for men (and women, too!). I deeply appreciate how Rhett consistently brings the focus of masculinity back to the relationship God the Father has with his Son, Jesus. After working with teenagers for the past twelve years, I could see this book becoming a great resource to give to guys as they head off to college.

Emily P. Freeman, author of *Grace for the Good Girl* and creator of the blog Chatting at the Sky

The issues that Rhett addresses have always been very complex to me, and I couldn't figure out how he was going to address them in one book! After sitting down to read the first chapter, I was moved by the mastery and talent of Rhett's insight and writing. This is a masterful book that outlines clear ways for men to grasp the possibilities and responsibilities to live our lives fully, through our brokenness—as God intended for us. I know every men's group that I am involved with now and in the future will see this book as a required reading resource.

Kary Miller, founder and principal of Whetstone Inc.

As a man, I am glad Rhett has written this book. With Rhett's background in psychology and his Christian worldview, I think this book is a must-read for men who want to know more about what lies inside.

Darrell Vesterfelt, president of Prodigal Magazine

Manhood in the church today is fraught with confusion from a variety of voices. Rhett Smith is a qualified guide to help remedy that. *What It Means to Be a Man* undermines stereotypes in church and society that ensnare men with false expectations and unhealthy souls. It offers a road map to spiritual healing that is simple in the reading and profound in the application. The small group guide alone is worth the price of the book.

Dale Fincher, author and president of Soulation (soulation.org)

With a unique perspective born of both his hard professional and personal work, Rhett Smith offers men "cairns for the journey" and a vision of masculinity that is missing in so many places today—not least the church. Rhett's own vulnerability, humility, and wisdom are rare in a younger leader. His wisdom and insight reveals a teacher's heart and healer's soul. There is much to learn here.

Tod Bolsinger, senior pastor of San Clemente Presbyterian Church, author of *It Takes a Church to Raise a Christian*

What It Means to Be a Man

God's Design for Us in
a World Full of Extremes
Rhett Smith

MOODY PUBLISHERS

CHICAGO

© 2013 by
RHETT SMITH

All Scripture quotations, unless otherwise indicated, are taken from the *Holy Bible, New International Version*®, NIV®. Copyright ©1973, 1978, 1984 by Biblica, Inc.™ Used by permission of Zondervan. All rights reserved worldwide. www.zondervan.com

Edited by Steve Lyon
Interior design: Smartt Guys design

All names have been changed to protect confidentiality. All scenarios are composite stories of counseling situations. Any similarity to actual sessions is purely coincidental.

All websites and phone numbers listed herein are accurate at the time of publication but may change in the future or cease to exist. The listing of website references and resources does not imply publisher endorsement of the site's entire contents. Groups and organizations are listed for informational purposes, and listing does not imply publisher endorsement of their activities.

Library of Congress Cataloging-in-Publication Data

Smith, Rhett.
   What it means to be a man : God's design for us in a world full of extremes / Rhett Smith.
      pages cm
   Includes bibliographical references.
   ISBN 978-0-8024-0668-2
   1. Men (Christian theology) I. Title.
   BT703.5.S57 2013
   248.8'42--dc23

                      2013003337

We hope you enjoy this book from Moody Publishers. Our goal is to provide high-quality, thought-provoking books and products that connect truth to your real needs and challenges. For more information on other books and products written and produced from a biblical perspective, go to www.moodypublishers.com or write to:

Moody Publishers
820 N. LaSalle Boulevard
Chicago, IL 60610

1 3 5 7 9 10 8 6 4 2

Printed in the United States of America

Thank you to my father, Tim—
you have always believed in me. It is through your life
and relationship with God I have learned what it means
to be a man. Thank you, Dad, for continually breathing
life into me on this journey.

Thank you to my daughter, Hayden, and son, Hudson—
you have always brought me great joy in being a father.

Thank you to my wife, Heather—
you are the biggest encouragement any husband could have.
Thanks for your constant belief in me. It is because of your
love and support a book like this even comes to fruition.

I'm forever thankful to God who loved me so much
that He sent His only Son to die on the cross for me . . .
in order that I may have life.

A good man leaves an inheritance to his children's children.
Proverbs 13:22

Contents

Foreword

My wife and I met and fell in love in Bible College. Not only did we fall in love with each other, we fell in love with the potential of what God could do through us as we served Him together in the local church.

Six months after we met, we got engaged. A year after our engagement, we got married and were ready to start our life together. I was twenty-one years old and my wife was twenty, and although we were young, we were in love and knew that our love for God and each other would sustain us.

I thought I knew what it meant to be a good husband. I was a good boyfriend and a really good fiancé, so being a good husband would be pretty easy. A few months after we married, my wife realized that she didn't have the flu; she was pregnant.

Being a new husband and now a near-future father challenged the version of manhood I had believed in. Being a man was more about my character than it was my age. There was a lot at stake now.

All of a sudden, being a man took on a whole new meaning for me. In a matter of months I would be responsible for raising a son to become a man. It was (and is) intimidating. I had no clue of what being a man was all about. I did what many great men before me have done . . . I faked it.

For the first ten years of my marriage and the first nine years of fatherhood, I just pretended like I knew what I was doing in living out my manhood. It wasn't until my marriage imploded and my wife and I came close to divorce that I began to truly understand what being a man is about. It wasn't until I was able to admit that I didn't know what I was doing that I was able to begin to learn and live out many of the principles of this book.

Now, sixteen years later we have three boys in our house and have several conversations a week about what it means to be a man. There are days I feel like an expert. There are still several days I feel like a failure in being a man and modeling for my boys what it means to be a man.

One thing I've noticed as I attempt to raise young men who love God and live an authentic life is that there are many competing messages of what manhood looks like. Becoming a godly man isn't easy. Understanding God's vision for manhood is intimidating. In my opinion, there aren't many people pointing the way for men who want to live out God's all on their life.

We are mostly comfortable in giving general guidelines on how to behave as a man, but don't like to talk about many issues of the heart that keep most men wondering if they are normal; if they are alone; if there is any hope of living out God's vision for their life as a man.

Our intentions aren't bad; it's just that the subject is intimidating. It is intimidating to talk about emotional wounds that many men have but have never expressed. It is hard to talk about lust and porn and sexual brokenness. It is not easy to discuss being known and being a person of truth and admitting weakness or depression or anxiety. It isn't easy to talk about openness and vulnerability and insecurity.

While it is difficult, the truth is that talking about these things doesn't make you less of a man; talking about them frees you up to become more of the man God created you to be. Many of the mistakes I have made as a husband, father, and Christ follower have come because I have avoided these heart transformative conversations and settled instead for trying to change my behavior.

That is why I am so thankful for Rhett Smith and this book you hold in your hands. This book takes the bold risk to go to places and discuss things with men that we need to talk about. This is a book that calls out the best in each of us and challenges us to not settle for the version of manhood our culture presents us.

This isn't a safe book. This book will challenge you to look at your life and your heart in a way that you may not have before. But if you will choose to go on the journey that Rhett calls you to, the identity and the value and the purpose you will find will be grounded in the loving grace of your heavenly Father.

I am praying for you as you go on this journey. It is a journey to real, authentic manhood that will leave you more in love with Jesus and more equipped to be the man that He longs for you to be.

Justin Davis

Coauthor of *Beyond Ordinary: When a Good Marriage Just Isn't Good Enough*
Cofounder of RefineUs Ministries

Introduction

You can't measure manhood
with a tape line around the biceps.[1]
Billy Sunday

In the early 1950s, Navy captain James Lovell was flying night-combat air patrol in an F2H Banshee off the coast of Japan. After completing his mission, he was scheduled to rendezvous with two other planes and return to the aircraft carrier USS *Shangri-La*. But the plane's Auto Direction Finder malfunctioned, and instead of directing him to the rendezvous and the carrier, it homed in on a signal coming from the coast of Japan. Suddenly a semi-routine flight became a frightful night for the pilot, now flying blind in stormy weather conditions. He lit up a board he invented to read various instruments in the cockpit, but it quickly shorted out, leaving him in complete darkness. He circled and circled, hoping to make sense of what was happening to him.

Then something remarkable happened. His eyes adjusted to the darkness, and in the sea below, he saw a "faint, greenish glow forming a shimmery trail in black water."[2] He realized it was the phosphorescent algae being churned up by the ship's screws. That faint trail of light led Captain Lovell all the way to the carrier where he landed safely.

When I first read of that story I was reminded of two things. One, as men we often find ourselves flying alone in the dark trying to understand what it means to be a man. Two, it's often in the darkness that a way forward slowly appears.

In the past, men in a community ushered boys into masculinity through rituals and rites. Unfortunately, some of them were violent and grotesque (i.e., ritualistic beatings and mutilation); others were more commonplace (getting your driver's license, dating, mowing the lawn, etc.). But as a growing body of literature on masculinity shows us, many boys today are stuck in adolescence because they miss those rituals. Others transition alone without the acknowledgment, affirmation, and blessing of other men who are crucial to breathing life into their emerging manhood.

The result is, like Captain Lovell, many of us are lost at sea not knowing how to generate change in our lives, let alone muster the ability to generate life-giving change with our friends and family. We find ourselves thinking . . .

"If someone could just tell me how to fix this, I would."

"I don't know what I want to do with my life."

"I don't want more responsibility."

"No one taught me how to be a man."

"I don't want to grow up."

"This isn't what I signed up for."

Our confusion can easily grow because, just when we think we have the answers, the questions change; or, we discover what defines a man in one generation changes in the next. For instance, many older men were raised to believe manhood means being strong and silent. Yet many younger men find the people they know longing for communication and connection. Add to that the sheer volume of books, papers, and research on the topic—each with a different take—and it's easy to understand why we're lost in the dark.

Over the last eighteen years, I've had the great privilege of working with boys and men in churches, universities, community mental health clinics, and private practice. I've learned, above all else, the "faint, greenish glow" that leads us home is God's role in our life. In other words, we have a choice to anchor our masculinity in either the defining values of the culture or the defining values of God. At times, there's agreement between the two; at other times, we must have the courage to walk the path God puts before us.

> *I've learned, above all else,* **the "faint, greenish glow"** *that leads us home* **is God's role in our life.**

Once that's settled, the other themes in this book will help you make the journey to manhood. That can be scary because God has a habit of calling us into the unknown. While there, it can seem like a wilderness. Yet it's where He often calls us into a deeper relationship with Him—and ultimately that's where our masculinity is defined.

That doesn't mean "one size fits all" regarding *how* masculinity looks for each of us. God chooses to relate to each one differently, depending on how He's made us. Therefore, we each express our masculinity differently. True, it may look similar to others, but it will have a uniqueness all its own.

Yet the *call* to manhood is the same regardless of race, color, language, culture, upbringing, or the life we currently lead. Our job is to live in an intimate relationship with God the Father and let our masculinity flow out of it. There, in that place, we will discover what it means to be a man.

How to Use This Book

When I lived in Pasadena, CA, one of my favorite runs was a 3.1 mile loop near the Rose Bowl. I'd start around the stadium and golf course, veer off the paved roads onto one of the many trails that emerge in the foothills of the San Gabriel Mountains, head through the Arroyo Seco, and then under the Colorado Street Bridge. I'd often come across 6"–12" stacks of rocks

We should think of these chapters as cairns *in our journey* toward manhood.

known as cairns[3] (a Scottish-Gaelic word), which were used as trail markers to warn of impending dangers or places where trails were not obvious.

We should think of these chapters as cairns in our journey toward manhood. If we pay attention, they'll help us successfully navigate its terrain and arrive safely at our destination. At the end of each chapter, I've included a challenge that will provide encouragement and guidance on what to do next. Also, consider reading the book with other men. Part of manhood is understanding the value of immersing ourselves in a life-breathing community of guys who share the journey with us. To make that easier, I've included a four-month study guide that includes questions, reflections, and exercises.

Thanks for allowing me to partner with you on this journey. My prayer is this book will be a hopeful and helpful guide as you explore what it means to be a man in your life and relationships.

Rhett Smith
November 12, 2012
McKinney, TX

Part One
Awareness

*As men, we need to be aware of the journey we are on
and how we have been and are being shaped . . .*

Archetypes
The Making of Men

*And out of darkness came the hands
that reach thro' nature, moulding men.*[1]
Alfred Lord Tennyson

I have always been intrigued by the Bible's account of David's encounter with Goliath. What little boy isn't immediately captured by the story of another little boy going to battle against a giant and slaying him with only a smooth rock and a slingshot? It's larger than life, one many of us identify with as we grew up. Every boy throws rocks and most dream about it, wondering, "Do I have what it takes to slay the giant?"

That's a question we still ask. Our giants may not come in the form of other men, but there are plenty of others we battle on a daily basis. That makes David's story an archetype we frame our lives around. After all, he was a man after God's own heart (1 Sam. 13:14; Acts 13:22).

The word *archetype* is taken from the combination of two Greek words: *arch* (meaning first), and *type* (meaning a model or mold).[2]

Every boy throws rocks and **most dream about it,** *wondering* **"Do I have what it takes to slay the giant?"**

"An archetype is a universally understood symbol, term, or pattern of behavior, a prototype upon which others are copied, patterned, or emulated."[3] In essence, archetypes are models we want to emulate. Whether we realize it or not, most of us constantly scan the horizon looking for one. If it resonates, it becomes the reference point for our masculinity. Though discovering the role of male archetypes in our life can be an insightful experience, we also want to avoid modeling our lives solely around them. There is potential danger that any model, even a biblical one, is prone to weakness and sin. David embodies several male archetypes (warrior, lover, king, and sage), and his sin with Bathsheba is a prime example of their unhealthy forms (2 Sam. 11–12).

The text starts with a telling statement: "In the spring, at the time when kings go off to war, David sent Joab out with the king's men and the whole Israelite army. They destroyed the Ammonites and besieged Rabbah. But David remained in Jerusalem" (11:1).

David is the king of Israel. God anointed him to bring peace and prosperity to the land. We get a glimpse of that in 2 Samuel 5:9–10: "David then took up residence in the fortress and called it the City of David. He built up the area around it, from the supporting terraces inward. And he became more and more powerful, because the Lord God Almighty was with him." But at this critical moment he chose to stay home when "kings go off to war," giving us a glimpse of his controlling and manipulative warrior side. A righteous warrior would have led his men into battle, putting his safety at risk for their good. By staying home, David chose self-interest over that of the kingdom and those who live in it.

As the text proceeds, we get a glimpse of his shadowy lover side. He lets passion turn to lust and commits adultery with Bathsheba. Then he shows us his shadowy king side by using his power to arrange Uriah's death, involving his commander Joab (unknowingly) in the plot. Finally, in an ironic twist, his shadowy sage (or prophet) side is exposed as Nathan reveals his sin, exposing the once eloquent author of God's Word with judgment from God's Word (2 Sam. 12:7).

> *In essence,* **archetypes are models we want to emulate.** *Whether we realize it or not,* **most of us** *constantly* **scan the horizon** *looking* **for one.** *If it resonates,* **it becomes the reference point for our masculinity.**

Male Archetypes

Recognition of male archetypes isn't limited to the Bible. There are a surprising number of Christian, secular, liberal, and conservative writers who discuss it—and they use many of the same terms. Some of the more common are warrior, king, sage (sometimes described as "magician"), and lover.[4] That's further proof they're images that have informed and shaped our perceptions of manhood.

The Big Four

As seen in David's life, archetypes have an unhealthy side. When a man accesses his immature or "shadowy" side, he is a boy, not a man. We'll touch briefly on those below—but also look at the positive side.

The King Archetype

As mature kings, we're secure. We're the source of order, and our actions sacrificially bring life to those around us. We encourage others to use their God-given talents and enable them to try things with a sense of confidence. When we're kings from an immature or shallow place, we can be tyrants, controlling those around us, always thinking about ways to exercise power over them.

The Warrior Archetype

As warriors, we live by a code. We act quickly with purpose and intention and sacrifice for our beliefs and those around us. It's the archetype we see most frequently in our culture, especially in our literature and movies, and it's the one most of us try to emulate. However, many are stuck on its shadowy side, which means being emotionally detached and quick to be aggressive and violent.

The Sage Archetype

When we're doing well as a sage, people come to us for advice and discernment. We speak truth to all who are willing to listen and, like Old Testament prophets, even those who aren't! We lovingly guide others and encourage them to be more Christlike. When we're behaving immaturely in this area, we can't be fully trusted because we manipulate others for our benefit.

The Lover Archetype

As mature lovers, we're full of life and passion. We're creative, think outside the box, and find solutions to problems in unique ways. We talk openly about our feelings. We bring life to others and emotionally connect with them. When we reflect this archetype from an immature or shadowy place, we pursue things that make us feel good about ourselves, often at others' expense. We seek our own gratification because it brings the instant pleasure and affirmation we long for. We're also prone to addictions to escape life and find relief from our pain.

Challenge

Now that you have had a glimpse of the four archetypes, sit down with a trusted friend, explain the positive and negative sides of each, and ask him which archetypes sound the most like you. Give him permission to let you know when you are accessing its positive and negative sides.

Extremes

A Tale of Two Men

> *Combine the extremes, and you*
> *will have the true center.*[1]
> **Karl Wilhelm Friedrich von Schlegel**

There is a powerful scene in the 1999 movie *Fight Club* in which the passive, nameless narrator (played by Edward Norton) realizes he and Tyler Durden, a tough, aggressive character (played by Brad Pitt), are the same people. It's a stunning moment of realization and one of the reasons so many men in our culture resonated with the film. I was twenty-four at the time and remember all of my male friends talking about it—and one had only to watch the news to see stories about "fight clubs" breaking out across the country.

The effect of the film still lingers. Three years ago there were several news stories about high school "fight nights" taking place in my hometown of Frisco, Texas.[2] Believe it or not, they were often held in private homes while parents watched and encouraged their sons and friends to duke it out. It's a *sad* reminder men are struggling to find their bearing between being too passive and too aggressive.

The Passive Man

John was a successful businessman with a wife and three kids and volunteered as a lay leader at his church. He came across as confident and in control. But after meeting him, he reminded me of a lot of men I work with—well-liked by others but almost impossible to get to know.

Underneath the "together" exterior, he was reeling because his life and relationships were coming apart at the seams. He and his wife had drifted apart, and she was increasingly impatient with his inability to connect emotionally with the family. When I explored that with him, he sat across from me, listless, almost in a daze. He couldn't describe what he was feeling except to say he was frustrated and didn't know what to do. "If she would just give me a list of what she wants, then I could do it. I could fix this."

I was amazed at how someone so outwardly successful was unable to be a life-giver to his family—that is, be their biggest cheerleader, bring out their natural strengths, allow them to be who God created them to be, and help them overcome obstacles. When a family enjoys a life-giving husband and father, they're at their best.

I probed more. "John, imagine it's a month from now. Changes have happened in your life and relationships . . . changes that signal you're headed in the right direction. . . . What would those look like?"

He looked at me for a little while and said, "I don't know."

No matter how many questions I asked, how many ways I tried to engage him, or how many times I encouraged him to experiment with changes, he seemed stuck and directionless.

John was a passive man.

If we're like him we're unable to create change and offer life-giving relationships to those around us. Our ability to see that is often obscured by statements like, "I work hard, I make a good living . . . I'm a good Christian guy, I go to church . . . my wife and kids have all they need and want . . . I don't beat them and I don't cheat on my wife . . . what else do they want!?" In other words, we believe what we're doing is all that's necessary—and if we realize change is needed we don't know how to bring it about.

The Aggressive Man

Chris owned and operated a successful advertising firm, was married with two kids, and volunteered much of his time in the men's ministry at church. His "go get 'em" attitude made it seem everything was going his way—which made a lot of men want to spend time with him.

Yet rage lurked just under his confident exterior. For Chris, manhood meant being tough and intimidating, and it made some people uneasy . . . especially his family. Ironically, an argument with his wife led him to start counseling with me. That said, he wasn't happy to be in my office and did everything he could to make me feel small (a common tactic). Aggression was the only emotion he knew how to express.

> *Men are* **struggling** *to find their bearing* **between being** *too* **passive and** *too* **aggressive.**

The Two Extremes

While there is a lot of room to live between the two extremes, many of us choose to live at one end or the other. In fact, if you listen closely to our wives, children, and friends, we're often described like this:

"He just sits there and says nothing when I talk to him or ask him a question."

"My dad comes home from work, eats dinner, and just retreats to the TV for the rest of the night. He doesn't engage us at all."

"He has no patience for our kids. As soon as he walks in the door he is angry if they aren't on their best behavior."

"We never do anything. We don't go out. We don't have many friends. I don't even know what he is excited about other than watching football all day."

"I want to connect with him on a deep level, but he doesn't seem capable of doing that. It's like he's lost somewhere inside his head. And when I do press him for conversation, he erupts as if what I'm asking is a huge inconvenience."

"Sometimes when I'm around my dad I don't feel very safe. I don't think he's going to hit me, but it seems as if he's always about to lose it . . . like he has no patience for my presence."

"We are all always walking on eggshells around him. It's so uncomfortable when he's around. We can't wait till he goes away on a business trip. When he's gone, then the house is calm and peaceful."

It doesn't help that movies and TV draw attention to both extremes, from the passive sitcom dad who is little more than the family joke, to the aggressive, big screen tough guy who destroys everyone in his path.

I've seen both played out more than I'd like to admit. Unfortunately, the church hasn't always been a place to see a balance between the two. The *passive* Christian guy doesn't seem to feel anything and can't affect change in his own life, let alone the lives of others. The *aggressive* Christian guy is tough and uses power and strength to broker relationships.

Though at opposite extremes, these men have a lot more in common than we think. They are stuck in one ideal of what it means to be a man and fail to give life to themselves and others.

The good news is **we don't have to live at either extreme . . . We can learn to be life-givers, encouraging** *those around us,* **confident** *in our approach to life, and* **supportive** *of those we care about.*

If we're passive, we withdraw and fail to encourage those we love in their pursuits. We don't model the confidence they need to feel secure. If we're aggressive, our anger sucks the life out the people around us, often causing them to walk on eggshells or withdraw completely.

The good news is we don't have to live at either extreme. God calls us to live our faith *between* these two unhealthy places. We don't have to terrorize *or* withdraw. We can learn to be life-givers, encouraging those around us, confident in our approach to life, and supportive of those we care about. When life frustrates us, we can handle things skillfully, knowing we've developed healthy ways to cope.

Challenge

I encourage you to honestly ask if you're too passive or aggressive. If not, great! If you are, what issues are you struggling with and how can you become more balanced?

Fathering

Breathing Life into the Son

*No good work is done anywhere
without aid from the Father of Lights.*[1]
C. S. Lewis

3

Derek Redmond couldn't believe it. Ninety seconds before his 400-meter qualifying heat in the 1988 Seoul Olympics, he was forced to withdraw with an injury to his Achilles tendon. Years of work, pain, and sacrifice instantly went up in smoke. He was devastated.

He endured eight operations in the years following and set his sights on the Barcelona Olympics in 1992. By the time they started, he was one of the fastest 400-meter runners in the world. He recorded the quickest qualifying time of the first round and cruised to an easy win in the quarter final.

I was seventeen that summer, heading into my senior year of high school. I loved track and field—I ran the 300-meter hurdles and was part of the 4x400 team—so I couldn't wait to hunker down on the couch one August afternoon for a long day of watching the

Olympics. It was pre-DVR days, so to avoid missing anything important I watched every track race. I was particularly excited about my favorite, the 400 meter because it's a combination of speed, power, and stamina. Like millions of fans, I wasn't prepared for what was about to unfold in the semifinals.

Redmond lined up in the starting blocks knowing he was favored to medal. When the starter's gun fired, he was up and running quickly, gaining momentum and looking fast over the first 100 meters. But at 150 meters his hamstring snapped like a worn rubber band and he quickly pulled up, clutching the back of his leg. He fell to the ground and put his hand over his face in agony—not just from the physical pain but the crushing realization his Olympic medal was gone.

As he lay on the track, everyone thought he was waiting for race officials to help him off. Yet in a courageous act of determination and perseverance, he stood up and began hobbling down the backstretch. As track officials came to his aid he brushed them aside, determined to finish the race. It was hard—and beautiful—to watch.

When male energy is absent, creation does not happen, *either in the human soul or in the world. . . .* **Without the father's energy, there is a void,** *an emptiness in the soul which* **nothing but that kind of energy can fill.**

Suddenly Derek's father, Jim, burst onto the track, pushing past everyone who tried to stop him. He ran to his son, leaned against him and . . . one painful step at a time . . . finished the race with him. The stadium flooded with a powerful sense of energy that compelled everyone to leap to their feet for a standing ovation.

Life-Giving Energy

In his book *The Wild Man's Journey*, Richard Rohr talks about the life-giving energy fathers give children (and what happens when they don't). He writes:

> When a father tells a child that he can do something, he can do it. I don't know why that is, except to say that there is some mysterious energy that passes from the male to his children. It is some sort of creative energy that can make things be when they are not, and without which things cannot come to be. When male energy is absent, creation does not happen, either in the human soul or in the world. Nurturance happens, support and love perhaps, but not that new "creation out of nothing" that is the unique prerogative associated with the masculine side of God . . . Without the father's energy, there is a void, an emptiness in the soul which nothing but that kind of energy can fill. I have seen it in too many people, men especially. It is a hollow yearning that feeds on praise incessantly and is never satisfied. It is a black hole that sucks in reward after reward and is never brightened by it. It becomes a nesting place of demons—of self-doubt, fear, mistrust, cynicism, and rage. And it becomes the place from which those demons fly out to devour others.[2]

As Rohr mentions, this energy is mysterious and powerful. It allows a son to move confidently and courageously into the world, full of life and able to give life to those around him. It reminds me of the scene in John 5 where Jesus' authority to heal on the Sabbath is challenged by religious leaders. He responds to them in verses 19–21:

> Jesus gave them this answer: "I tell you the truth, the Son can do nothing by himself; he can do only what he sees his

Father doing, because whatever the Father does the Son also does. For the Father loves the Son and shows him all he does. Yes, to your amazement he will show him even greater things than these. For just as the Father raises the dead and gives them life, even so the Son gives life to whom he is pleased to give it."

Jesus said He could do nothing by Himself, but only what He saw His Father doing. The Father brought life and the Son did the same. In the same way, when we follow Christ we give life to our sons. Larry Crabb in *The Silence of Adam* puts it this way: "A godly father speaks three messages to his son: 1. 'It can be done. 2. You're not alone. 3. I believe in you.'"[3] Without that message, sons move into the world and find they do not know who they are or what to do.

Giving that kind of energy to our sons doesn't require a "big moment." It can happen in the everyday occurrences of life. Recently I was watching my two-year-old son, Hudson, jump on the trampoline while he laughed and called out "Dad . . . watch me . . . watch me Dad . . . watch me!" I know he could have had fun doing it without me. But there was special delight in knowing his father was enjoying it and giving his approval. In that moment, he drew energy and strength from me—and I was delighted to give it.

Dads, let me encourage all of us to actively engage with our sons on a daily basis. We don't have to have all the answers. We just need to be available and willing to help as they discover each new stage of life. More importantly, we need to introduce them to God at an early age, teaching them how to have a daily relationship with Him. When they see how we trust Him—and how He boldly leads us into the world—they'll be inspired to do the same.

Father Wound/Father Hunger/Fatherlessness

Many men I've worked with have a longing for the father they never had—the man who should have taught them how to fix and build things, throw a football, tie a tie, cook a meal, and drive a car. They've had to figure it out on their own. That can be true even if our dads *were* around. Some, while physically present, weren't actively engaged in our lives, so our desire for fatherly love was never satisfied.

Giving that kind of energy *to our sons* doesn't require a "big moment." It can happen *in the* everyday *occurrences of life.*

If that describes you, look around at the men in your life. Is there someone who could mentor you—who could help you enjoy the benefit of a positive role model? If so, reach out to him and enjoy what he gives you and teaches you about being a life-giver.

Challenge

If you're a father, find time each day to engage with your son. One day it might be five minutes asking him about his day; the next, thirty minutes kicking a soccer ball back and forth. Whatever it is, be consistent and engage.

If you're not a father, look around your community and find a male you can spend weekly time with. It could be over a cup of coffee, a friendly morning run, or a prayer time. Again, be consistent and engaged—and enjoy being a life-giver to someone in need!

Part Two
Honesty

As men, we need to be honest about the things we are and have been struggling with . . .

Depression
Trapped in Our Anger

Being a man can be hazardous to your health,
especially when you have to maintain your
masculine identity at all costs.[1]
Archibald Hart

In a scene from the 1997 movie *Good Will Hunting*, math genius Will (Matt Damon) describes his foster father's abuse to his therapist, Sean (Robin Williams). As the questions probe more deeply Will becomes more agitated, until finally, when it seems he can't take another minute, his anger gives way to crying. That's when Sean embraces him, comforting him with these words: "It's not your fault . . . it's not your fault . . . it's not your fault!"[2] The scene is a powerful example of how anger masks sadness which masks depression—something I'm continually reminded of in my work with men.

Admitting we're depressed is tricky. Just mention the word and many men recoil, looking at me as if I'm insane. We fail to recognize it often hides behind coping mechanisms like success, money, sex, alcohol, violence, and sports. The trick is to pull back the layers and masks we use to disguise it, as authors like Parker Palmer,[3] Archibald Hart,[4] and Terence Real[5] remind us.

In *I Don't Want to Talk About It*, Real uncovers why we hide our depression. We begin life with as many feelings and emotions as girls, but as we age we begin hearing a different message.[6] Our fathers, mothers, teachers, coaches, and friends tell us things like, "Stop crying!" and "Don't be a wuss!" and "You're okay . . . pick yourself up! Be a man!" In other words, it's no longer safe to be emotional. If we want to test this, pay attention to the messages you give your son versus the messages you give your daughter. Or if we're a coach, mentor, or youth pastor, think about the messages we convey to boys that encourage them to just "suck it up."

Real writes:

> One of the ironies about men's depression is that the very forces that help create it keep us from seeing it. Men are not supposed to be vulnerable. Pain is something we are to rise above. He who has been brought down by it will most likely see himself as shameful, and so, too, may his family and friends, even the mental health profession. Yet I believe it is this secret pain that lies at the heart of many of the difficulties in men's lives.[7]

He also mentions aggressiveness and violence—and they're such major issues in our society I'd like to focus there. Though we'd like to think differently, God never made us to stuff our feelings. If we do long enough, we *will* find other ways to express them—and for many that means becoming aggressive and violent. Video games, sports, and fighting are some of the culturally condoned ways we do it.

Pressed to the Ground

For many of us, the journey to healing and wholeness is to admit we are depressed and discover what God is revealing in the midst of it. A lot of men will do anything to avoid difficulty, often choosing to numb pain with medications, alcohol, drugs, sex, and violence. Yet what if the feelings and emotions we've been suppressing actually lead to life? What if depression is a *gift* that helps us conquer the emotions that weigh us down? Parker Palmer, in his eloquent account of his depression, writes the following:

> **Admitting we're depressed** *is tricky. Just mention the word and* **many men recoil, looking at me as if I'm insane.**

> After hours of careful listening, my therapist offered an image that helped me eventually reclaim my life. "You seem to look upon depression as the hand of an enemy trying to crush you," he said. "Do you think you could see it instead as the hand of a friend, pressing you down to the ground on which it is safe to stand?"

> Amid the assaults I was suffering, the suggestion that depression was my friend seemed impossibly romantic, even insulting. But something in me knew that down, down to the ground, was the direction of wholeness, thus allowing that image to begin its slow work of healing me.

> I started to understand that I had been living an ungrounded life, living at an altitude that was inherently unsafe. The problem with living at high altitude is simple: when we slip, as we always do, we have a long, long way to fall, and the landing may well kill us. The grace of being pressed down to

the ground is also simple: when we slip and fall, it is usually not fatal, and we can get back up.[8]

"The grace of being pressed down . . ." In our darkest nights of depression it's the hand of God pressing us down . . . an act of grace leaving us grounded and more whole.

You may anger easily and struggle with aggression and violence. It may have led to physical altercations with strangers, friends, or family. Even if it hasn't, you can be fooled into thinking since you don't abuse your wife or kids you're not depressed. Yet complacency is often the first step toward depression. Don't let that happen to you. Be willing to seek the help you need before it shows itself in damaging ways.

"The grace of being pressed down. . ." *In our darkest nights of depression* **it's the hand of God pressing us down. . .** *an act of grace* **leaving us grounded and more whole.**

If you've admitted the problem and are seeking help, you may still be depressed—for a while. I applaud the courage you're showing in hanging in there and trust you'll successfully navigate depression's dark waters and come out in the light. Again, Palmer writes, "Though I recommend it to no one—and I do not need to, for it arrives unbidden in too many lives—depression compelled me to find the river of life hidden beneath the ice."[9]

Challenge

If you're angry and aggressive, realize it may be a mask for depression. It's okay to admit that—and that you aren't feeling as strong as you could be. Talk with another man in your life, with your church community, or a professional counselor. As you plumb the depths of your feelings, you'll find new life emerging out of the darkness. And you'll have the satisfaction of showing your family, friends, and other men anger isn't the pathway to manhood.

Silence

The Relational Abyss

*What we've got here is
a failure to communicate.*[1]
Cool Hand Luke

5

"**I** just want you to bring me in on the process! I have no idea what is going on inside your head. Just talk to me!" Those words came from an exasperated wife sitting in my office, staring at her husband. He sat in silence not knowing what to say—something we men are famous for.

When we don't communicate with important people in our lives, a void grows, and if words don't fill it the void gets larger. In counseling, couples in that situation often sit on my couch with space between them, symbolizing the void. Sometimes there's nothing in the space; at others, a pillow, purse, or another object. That's when I tell the husband, "When you can't communicate with your wife it's like there's a balloon between you. Each moment of silence fills it with more air and it pushes you away from each other. Eventually you realize just how far apart and disconnected

When you don't communicate, your wife has *no option but to put words in the void to make sense of things.* She may be accurate—or she may not be. But she's *left having to be* the only life-giver, *which is* what you were also created to do.

you've become—and that can be overwhelming."

More often than not, he pays attention. So I continue. "When you don't communicate, your wife has no option but to put words in the void to make sense of things. She may be accurate—or she may not be. But she's left having to be the only life-giver, which is what you were also created to do."

We get an important glimpse of that role in Genesis 2:19. In caring for the garden of Eden, one of Adam's first tasks was to name the animals. In essence, by naming them he fulfills his role as a life-giver.

In the fall, Adam faltered badly, something Larry Crabb points out in his wonderful book *The Silence of Adam*. He should have confronted the serpent but instead he is silent. Crabb sees this theme of masculine silence play out through the next forty-seven chapters of Genesis.[2]

Perhaps we're more like Adam than we care to admit. Instead of being men who live out the God-bearing image He's placed within us, we remain silent versus speaking into the void to care for, connect with, and protect our wives. When we're silent, we bring chaos and calamity on the scene. Crabb says, "My silence asks my wife to step into the confusion of my life. It requires her to pursue me in every interaction."[3]

Uncovering Our Silence

We can feel we're behind the curve when it comes to knowing what to say to our wife, girlfriend, family member, or friend. We want to breathe life into our relationships but don't know how. Take heart. There are a lot of us in the same boat. Psychologist and researcher Terence Real writes:

> Many boys are taught to be so proficient at burying their exuberance that they manage to bury it even from themselves. Recent research indicates that in this society most males have difficulty not just in expressing, but even in identifying their feelings. The psychiatric term for this impairment is alexithymia and psychologist Ron Levant estimates that close to eighty percent of men in our society have a mild to severe form of it.[4]

I'm not suggesting men constantly share all their feelings, because there are times when silence is important. As Proverbs 17:28 reminds us, "Even a fool is thought wise if he keeps silent, and discerning if he holds his tongue." But Ecclesiastes 3:7 also says there is "a time to be silent and a time to speak." To understand the balance, we should think about how we cope with our feelings. For instance, if we choose silence but withdraw, stew, or pout, it should tip us off to share our feelings in a healthy way.

We can **recover our role** *as* **life-givers,** *too.*

Learning how to do that is easier than we might think. When I counsel men on this issue I show them a list of feelings and say, "If you aren't sure how you feel, look at some of these words and tell me which you experience the most." Most men can—and that helps them affirm what they've always thought about themselves but have been unable to communicate.

Adam may have failed as a life-giver during the temptation in Genesis 3, but he found his voice again and named Eve (Gen. 3: 20). We can recover our role as life-givers to our wives, too. Like my client, they desire us to fill the void and bring them into the process. Our words don't have to be perfect or eloquent. Sometimes, one word gets the ball rolling. At others, a sentence like, "I felt devalued at work today," or "I feel disconnected from you lately," will do.

Our sons need to know it's okay to express emotion, so when they're husbands they'll give life to their wives. "Son, sometimes I feel I'm not good enough around others at work, and I wonder if you feel that way around your peers or around me?" is a powerful investment in his life—and hers.

Challenge

As men created in God's image, we're given tools to breathe life into our relationships by sharing our feelings. Who needs to hear from you right now? Who needs you to bring them in on the process? I encourage you to start communicating with those you love today. It takes practice, but you'll quickly notice your spouse, children, coworkers, and friends responding positively.

Stuck

Moving Out of Your Box

6

*If it can't be fixed by duct tape
or WD-40, it's a female problem.*[1]
Comedian Jason Love

My wife, Heather, and I started dating as I finished my master of divinity degree at Fuller Seminary. It took five long years, and I thought I was ready to tackle any theological or ministry issue. I knew how to read Greek and Hebrew, discuss church history, parse the finer points of theology, write sermons, and do a lot of other things. I was confident I had everything I needed for the college ministry at Bel Air Presbyterian Church.

But I was inadequate in one important area of life—my dating relationship with Heather. Though I was constantly affirmed in my ministry, I quickly discovered the seminary tool belt wasn't of much use to me relationally. I felt unprepared and impotent.

That's what happens when we operate out of what Larry Crabb calls "recipe theology."[2] In other words, as long as there is a formula for managing relationships we're fine. It allows us to operate in what he calls our "boundaries of competence."[3] The problem with that mindset is relationships aren't designed to be managed.

Here's what I mean: Imagine a square. Inside it, write down the things you're competent at—work, hobbies, travel, sports, education, making money, and whatever else comes to mind. Crabb believes (as I do) we often feel most competent at work. That does not mean it's always easy, but it is the place we have the tools to get the job done successfully.

Some of us *will even* **abandon our families** *emotionally and physically* **to stay in a world where we feel** *more* **successful** *and* **appreciated.**

Imagine what it feels like when you've done a good job. Are you affirmed by others? Do you feel competent? Needed? Wanted? If the answer is yes, work is a boundary of competence for you.

Now focus on what's *outside* the square: family relationships. Rather than simply fix and solve a problem, this world requires us to actively engage by being curious, asking questions, and learning to listen (versus plugging into the TV or the Internet). We need to remember Paul's words in Ephesians 5:31–32, "For this reason a man will leave his father and mother and be united to his wife, and the two will become one flesh. This is a profound mystery—but I am talking about Christ and the church." To fully engage that mystery requires a different set of tools and skills than we often use.

That can be a fearful thing. It pushes on the anxiety that we can't remedy things at a moment's notice. Rather than face that, many of us choose to operate with the same tool belt we use at work. That's why some of us bring work home. If we keep checking texts, replying to emails, and taking phone calls, we're effective and successful. Some of us will even abandon our families emotionally and physically to stay in a world where we feel more successful and appreciated. But that just helps us avoid the reality that relationships are hard and it takes courage to engage in them.

To be sure, there are situations where things need to get done and issues need to be addressed. Therefore, I'm not suggesting we get rid of our "fix it" tool, but that patience and listening need to be part of our tool belt. As we spend time using them, we'll develop even more tools to navigate the mystery of the relationships God has put in our lives.

When I was growing up I'd go to my dad when I needed help with a problem. At times, he knew how to help me—at others, he didn't. But I always knew he was there ready to enter my mess at a moment's notice. That taught me I didn't need to tackle life alone and that men are there for the people in their lives even when there's not a quick fix to the problem. If we do our part, we can trust God to do His and bring about the resolution in His time and in His way.

Challenge

Think about what it's like when you can't fix a problem or solve some type of issue with your family. Do you get uncomfortable? Do you feel inadequate? When that happens do you withdraw or shut down? Do you get angry? If so, ask God for His help to be patient, listen, ask questions, and trust Him (rather than feeling you have to fix things).

Part Three

Openness

As men, we need to continually risk being open in our relationships . . .

Encounter
Shaped by the Other

7

All actual life is encounter.[1]
Martin Buber

There is a scene in the Bible I've been drawn to more than any other in the last few years. I've talked about it in my other writings because it's captured my imagination, helping me move into the world with courage and confidence. It teaches us the foundation of our identity is our relationship with our heavenly Father rather than work, money, fame, and success. By "identity" I mean the core beliefs around which we organize our life and that give us meaning and purpose. That starts with the compelling truth that "if anyone is in Christ, he is a new creation; the old has gone, the new has come!" (2 Cor. 5:17). It reaches into every thought and action and holds the promise of living differently. Once we understand that, we can comprehend the impact of our relationship with our Father.

The scene I'm talking about is Jesus' baptism (Matt. 3:16–17,

Mark 1:9–11, and Luke 3:21–22). As you read it, think about what resonates regarding your identity as a man.

"At that time Jesus came from Nazareth in Galilee and was baptized by John in the Jordan. Just as Jesus was coming up out of the water, he saw heaven being torn open and the Spirit descending on him like a dove. And a voice came from heaven: 'You are my Son, whom I love; with you I am well pleased.'" (Mark 1:9–11 NIV 2011).

By "identity" *I mean the* **core beliefs** *around which we organize our life and* **that give us meaning and purpose.**

Jesus' identity wasn't grounded in the things He did or was about to do. It was not in His role as a miracle worker or faith healer. His identity and worth were rooted in His Father's unchangeable love. He was *God's Son*—and the same is true for us. True, we develop intimacy and closeness with Him through our obedience. But our intrinsic worth as His children is not changed by what we do or fail to do. He loves us because we are His children.

Encounter of the Holy Other

Jesus' relationship with His Father gave meaning to His identity and clarity to His purpose. It gave Him the ability to move into the world with courage and confidence. That was critical, because after His baptism He was tempted to turn stone into bread, throw Himself off the highest part of the temple, and worship Satan (Matt. 4:1–11, Mark 1:12–13, and Luke 4:1–13).

In the same way, our relationship with God our Father is the anchor that keeps us from temptations to look at other things like success at work (including praise, money, power, or status), sports, fantasy sports leagues, alcohol, drugs, sex, and pornography for a sense of identity. It also allows us to fulfill His purposes—note that immediately following His temptation, Jesus moved out of the desert to begin the Father's work of calling disciples and preaching.

Encounter with the Not-Me

Though our identity and purpose is first and foremost in God, our earthly father plays a significant role in shaping that. Matthew 1:18–25 gives us a powerful glimpse of that truth. Jesus' earthly father, Joseph, could have left Mary and his unborn son, but he chose to listen to God's word and stay. Jesus grew up knowing Joseph loved and accepted Him, and that He was worthy because He was His father's son. Richard Rohr says, "The father is the first encounter with not-me. His acceptance or rejection is our first clue as to whether the outer world can be trusted. . . . It is our first experience of election, of being chosen."[2] In other words, His early feelings of acceptance started with His earthly father and continued with His heavenly Father.

> **Jesus' relationship with His Father gave meaning *to* His identity *and* clarity *to* His purpose. *It gave Him* the ability to move *into the world* with courage and confidence.**

If you had a father like Joseph, be thankful. It's a gift many men never received. If you didn't, be encouraged your heavenly Father loves you in ways no earthly father can. He has elected and chosen you to be His child and wants to be the greatest source of love in your life. One of the ways He does that is through the care you receive from friends, coworkers, roommates, extended family, or your small group.

We will always face the challenge to abandon our identity in

God our Father and place it in things we believe will make us feel wanted, needed, and accepted. Yet we must cling to the belief we are deeply loved by God. As Henri Nouwen so necessarily reminds us, "Being the Beloved constitutes the core truth of our existence."[3] Trust in that enables us to live out His purpose for our lives rather than the fleeting purposes of a misplaced identity.

Challenge

What things have you built your identity on—God our Father, or what you can do and achieve? Do you struggle with placing your identity in things like work (praise, money, power, and status), sports, sports fantasy leagues, alcohol, drugs, sex, and pornography? Ask God to help you remove these struggles so you can find your identity in His love for you.

Vulnerability
Opening Ourselves Up

8

To love at all is to be vulnerable.[1]
C. S. Lewis

In March 2001, I lived in Antigua, Guatemala. As part of Semana Santa (which is Spanish for "Holy Week"), I visited the stations of the cross in a local church. At one station, I was mesmerized by a statue of Jesus. He was sitting with His chin on His hand and a deep look of contemplation on His face. I'd never seen anything like it—and I took a picture of it which sits on my desk to this day.

Later that night I talked about the statue with the grandmother of my host family. I said, "I wonder what He is thinking about?" She immediately responded, "La Passion," which means, "The Passion," the term used for the events surrounding Jesus' betrayal, trial, execution, and crucifixion.

As I thought about it I realized His vulnerability is what captured me—that double-edged sword that positions us for both connection and disconnection. On the one hand, it means giving away our power, which leaves us open to all types of physical, emotional, mental, and spiritual pain. It can be experienced in a number of ways such as shame, criticism, attacks, and disconnection. But on the other hand, it allows us to experience the deepest and most intimate relationships. That's why the person we love most deeply and experience the most life-giving intimacy with is also the one who can hurt us more than anyone else. We cannot experience pain without vulnerability—but we can't experience connection without it either.

Jesus lived with excruciating vulnerability.[2] For three years, He walked closely with His disciples, knowing they would betray Him.[3] And on the dark day of His crucifixion, He yielded His power and hung on the cross with His arms outstretched to a world who rejected Him. The essential question is "What can we learn from His example?"

We cannot **experience pain without vulnerability—** *but we can't* **experience connection without it** *either.*

Early in life we're taught power is the currency we need to survive. We learn to spend it on the playground and the playing field; and we take it into the competitive world of corporate boardrooms, adult relationships, and even the church. (I've spent my entire life behind the scenes in churches, and letting go of power is as big a struggle there as it is many other places.)

Yet to follow Christ we must engage others with our arms and hands spread out, free to give and receive from them. That's not easy because we want to huddle around things like success, money, sex, strength, careers, and sports which can get in the way of our relationships with God and others. But as the apostle Paul reminds us in Philippians 2:1–8, Christlikeness requires a self-emptying that only happens when we let go of those things and move toward greater vulnerability.

> If you have any encouragement from being united with Christ, if any comfort from his love, if any fellowship with the Spirit, if any tenderness and compassion, then make my joy complete by being like-minded, having the same love, being one in spirit and purpose. Do nothing out of selfish ambition or vain conceit, but in humility consider others better than yourselves. Each of you should look not only to your own interests, but also to the interests of others.
>
> Your attitude should be the same as that of Christ Jesus:
> Who, being in very nature God,
> did not consider equality with God something to be grasped,
> but made himself nothing,
> taking the very nature of a servant,
> being made in human likeness.
> And being found in appearance as a man,
> he humbled himself
> and became obedient to death—
> even death on a cross! (Phil. 2:1–8)

Christlikeness *requires a* **self-emptying** *that only happens* **when we let go** *of those things* **and move toward greater vulnerability.**

Men throughout Scripture have learned that lesson. Jacob used his power to deceive and steal. He became a man on the run, living on his own terms. God encountered him when he was most vulnerable, wrestling with him in a struggle not for power but for intimacy (Gen. 32:22–32).[4] By yielding, he experienced greater closeness to God and reconciliation with his brother, Esau. He let go of control and was free to experience God in a new way.

The apostle Peter learned about vulnerability, too. In the closing chapter of John's gospel, Jesus reinstates him in ministry after he denied Him. The excruciating vulnerability he required of Peter is haunting.

> "I tell you the truth, when you were younger you dressed yourself and went where you wanted; but when you are old you will stretch out your hands, and someone else will dress you and lead you where you do not want to go." Jesus said this to indicate the kind of death by which Peter would glorify God. Then he said to him, "Follow me!" (John 21:18–19)

All of us must learn following God requires complete vulnerability, allowing all the things we cling to for security to fall at our feet. Only then can Christ truly lead us—sometimes to places we don't want to go.

Challenge

Identify a relationship where you need to be more vulnerable. You may need to take down a wall created with anger, distance, or silence. Or you may need to resist the temptation to withdraw in fear. For example, tell your wife how you have tried to cope with an issue in your marriage in an unhealthy way (i.e., withdrawing, getting angry, or pouting). Or tell a close friend what his friendship means to you. You may need to express your vulnerability to someone through asking forgiveness for something you have done to them.

Intimacy

Being Known

For Thou hast made us for Thyself and
our hearts are restless till they rest in Thee.[1]
Augustine

Tom and Beth had been married less than a year when they came
to me for therapy. After saying hello and taking our seats, we
sat in silence for a few moments. Finally I said, "So after ten months
of marriage I imagine something has happened you need some help
with?" After a bit more silence, Tom shared they dated for two years
and were engaged for another and had waited for sex until they were
married. On their wedding night, he was unable to perform like he
and Beth hoped, leaving him disappointed and impotent.

I wasn't surprised the unfulfilled expectations and disappointment of their wedding night left them hurt, disconnected, and unable to talk about it. That's not uncommon. Many couples tell me
stories of unfulfilled expectations and desires that go all the way
back to their first or early sexual encounters.

Though we often think of impotency in the context of our

sexuality, many of us feel impotent in other areas, too. We typically react in one of several ways. We try to control people close to us to demonstrate how strong we are. We bury ourselves in work or a hobby we're competent in. We detach from people we feel powerless around, because being close is a painful reminder of our ineffectiveness. Or we indulge in other relationships with people who make us feel good about ourselves.

In retelling the myth of Narcissus, Terence Real points out Narcissus was immobilized because he was dependent on his own image.[2] In other words, he had to manage how others saw him out of fear he would fail or disappoint them if they really knew him. That's why many of us move into pornography, love addictions, and affairs. These forms of escape numb us because the other person reflects back to us how we imagine ourselves to be. As long as that keeps happening, the escape works. But if not, failure and disappointment ensue and we scramble around looking for someone else to prop us up. If we can't find that person, we move away from intimacy because it strikes at the heart of one of our biggest fears, which is being vulnerable. Real notes boys are granted their manhood status by turning their backs on vulnerability.[3] Yet it's the one thing we need if we hope to experience love, sex, and intimacy.

> **Narcissus ... *had to* manage how others saw him** *out of fear he would* **fail or disappoint them** *if they* **really knew him.**

Intimacy with God

Our ability to experience love and intimacy with others flows out of our intimacy with God. As we learned in chapter seven, our identity isn't rooted in what we do but the vulnerability and acceptance we have as God's sons. To put it another way, our identity isn't built on our image being reflected *back* to us but the image of the Father flowing *through* us. The intimacy of that relationship is the blueprint for how we relate to others.

How that applies to our relationships with other men can be confusing. Yet the gospel of John provides us with two powerful examples. They show us how Jesus related to His closest friends, the disciples. Both examples occurred during the meal He shared with them before His crucifixion. The first was when He washed their feet—an incredible act of vulnerability and intimacy.

> It was just before the Passover Feast. Jesus knew that the time had come for him to leave this world and go to the Father. Having loved his own who were in the world, he now showed them the full extent of his love. The evening meal was being served, and the devil had already prompted Judas Iscariot, son of Simon, to betray Jesus. Jesus knew that the Father had put all things under his power, and that he had come from God and was returning to God; so he got up from the meal, took off his outer clothing, and wrapped a towel around his waist. After that, he poured water into a basin and began to wash his disciples' feet, drying them with the towel that was wrapped around him. (John 13:1–5)

When I was twenty, my brother and I served with a ministry that served children living barefoot in the dumps of Tijuana, Mexico. [4] One day the director of the ministry took us into a private tent near the dump. [5] Inside, about a hundred boys were waiting to receive their weekly showers—but their feet needed to be washed first and we were assigned the task. Our instructions? "No gloves. Just use your hands and a cloth. And look each boy in the eye as you wash his feet." It was one of the most powerful moments of vulnerability and intimacy I've had with another male—and it gave me a fresh perspective on the profound model of love Jesus' foot washing gives us.

Ask Him *to guide you in* **letting go** *of your* **self-identity and resting** *in the* **knowledge you are His son and He loves you.**

The second example occurred after the foot washing. Jesus informed the disciples one of them would betray Him. They were stunned—and curious who it could be. Since they were seated on the floor around a table just a few inches off the ground, John was able to lean against Jesus to find out more. It was a great sign of their closeness—and the intimacy *we* can have with Him: "One of them, the disciple whom Jesus loved, was reclining next to him. Simon Peter motioned to this disciple and said, 'Ask him which one he means.' Leaning back against Jesus, he asked him, 'Lord, who is it?'" (13:23–25).

How would you describe your intimacy with others? Maybe you're like Narcissus, demanding people hold up an idealized image of who you are and detaching if they don't. Maybe you long to connect with your wife but are afraid of failure. You may want to be open with your kids but are afraid you'll disappoint them. Maybe you desire great friendships with other men but are afraid of coming across as weak. Perhaps God feels very distant and you doubt He'll ever accept you for who you are.

Whatever the status of your relationships, start by being

vulnerable with God. He knows the state of your heart and your relationship with Him. Be honest. Ask Him to guide you in letting go of your self-identity and resting in the knowledge you are His son and He loves you. Tell Him you need help understanding the barriers that keep you from the intimate relationships you want. He may use someone else to help, so don't resist if He brings that person your way.

Challenge

Do you have an intimate relationship with God that allows you to be intimate with others—or are you too dependent on the image your spouse, family, or friends have of you? Practice two things today: One, ask God to reveal how to have a deeper relationship with Him, and reflect on one of the two passages in John for His insights. Two, focus daily on the times you are too dependent on others' views of you. When you catch yourself doing that, ask Him to help you be more dependent on His view of you.

Part Four
Movement

*As men, we need to live in a way that allows us
and others to move forward with growth . . .*

Re ceiving

Taking Care of Ourselves

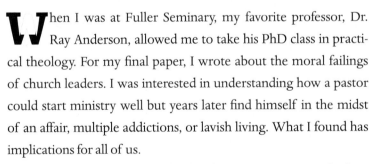

We don't forget that we are Christians.
We forget that we are human, and that
one oversight alone can debilitate the
potential of our future.[1]
Wayne Cordeiro

When I was at Fuller Seminary, my favorite professor, Dr. Ray Anderson, allowed me to take his PhD class in practical theology. For my final paper, I wrote about the moral failings of church leaders. I was interested in understanding how a pastor could start ministry well but years later find himself in the midst of an affair, multiple addictions, or lavish living. What I found has implications for all of us.

In a nutshell, those who fell failed to pay attention to the four core areas of self-care: physical, emotional, mental, and spiritual.[2] They neglected their bodies, often overworking, not eating well, and not exercising. Their spiritual life faltered because they substituted prayer and silence with God with the demands of a hectic schedule. They invested less in mental activities such as reading books, attending workshops, and being involved in retreats. Finally,

We care for ourselves *not because we are selfish but* **so we can give life to others.** *Otherwise,* **we suck the life out of people around us.**

they disconnected from people close to them—from their wives (which in many cases led to an affair) to men in the church who could have kept them accountable.

Pastors aren't the only ones who need to exercise self-care. Most of us are notoriously bad at it, often forfeiting our health and relationships to prove we're tough and able to pull ourselves up by our bootstraps. That's why "self-care" isn't something we resonate with. It makes us think of our eyes covered with cucumber slices while waiting for a pedicure, or engaging in some sort of weird new age practice.

I'm here to tell you it's none of those things. Self-care is "One's understanding and behavior that helps to build a healthy body, mind, and spirit for himself and others."[3] We care for ourselves not because we are selfish but so we can give life to others. Otherwise, we suck the life out of people around us.

You may wonder if the Bible has anything to say about the issue. I believe it does. Note Luke 2:52: "And Jesus grew in wisdom (mental) and stature (physical), and in favor with God (spiritual) and men (relational)"—(words in parenthesis, mine). Like Jesus, we want to grow and mature in these areas so we can love God, ourselves, and our neighbors (Luke 10:27). All four areas of self-care work together and are important for our overall health, so let's talk briefly about each.

Growing in Wisdom

When we are intentional about this aspect of life we practice things that keep us mentally sharp, stimulate our mind, and increase our level of discernment. It could be taking a class or engaging in continued training in our profession. Or it could mean seeking the help of a trusted friend or counselor to better navigate struggles we face. This is an important aspect of self-care because it often guides many other decisions we make in life. When we don't act wisely, many areas of our life suffer.

Growing in Stature

Though the apostle Paul reminds us in 1 Timothy 4:8 that "physical training is of some value, but godliness has value for all things, holding promise for both the present life and the life to come," poor health can contribute to poor decisions in other areas. When I'm tired due to lack of rest or feel sluggish because I haven't worked out, one of the last things I feel like doing is spending time with God.

Growing in Favor with God

This means being clearly focused on connecting with God. There are a number of ways to do that: prayer, silence in order to clearly discern what God is saying to us, or attending a Bible study. Many of us find it helpful to create a specific time and space for these things, for example, retreating to a favorite chair at a certain time of the day to connect with God. Or planning a monthly or yearly retreat to be alone and spend extra time in prayer and silence. I also know several men who get away on a yearly retreat with one another.

Another essential way to connect with God is by observing the Sabbath. It's a tangible way to express trust He'll care for us even when we're not working—and it's grounded in the confidence He loves us for who we are (i.e., His sons) not what we do for Him (See Mark 1:9–11. See chapter seven also).

Growing in Favor with Man

Being intentional here means deepening the emotional connection we have with others. For instance, we can plan a weekly date night with our wife. Rather than talk about the household (i.e., kids, budget, planning events, work, or gossiping), we should focus on getting to know her. As we learned in chapter eight, we should also share how we feel—including things that excite us and where we're struggling.

Other ideas are: getting coffee every week with a close friend to share the highs and lows of our week; involving our kids in a service project; making a commitment to control our temper on the basketball court; and resolving conflicts at work in a godly way.

Self-care is like the tires on a car. It's important to keep the right amount of air pressure in them and rotate them at regular intervals. We also need to avoid nails and other sharp objects that might tear them apart. If we do, the tires will have a long life and keep our car running smoothly. In the same way, maintaining the four components of self-care helps us navigate life more smoothly. That's especially true when we run into anxiety, depression, and stress. If unhealthy coping behaviors creep in, it's a good sign our self-care is lacking and steps should be taken to correct the imbalance.

Challenge

Are you intentional about developing these four areas of self-care? What's one practice in each area you can begin this week?

Giving
Returning Home to Community

*Finally, the hero is a hero precisely
because he knows how to re-integrate
within the community.*[1]
Richard Rohr

'n her 2010 book *Unbroken: A World War II Story of Survival, Resilience, and Redemption*, author Lauren Hillenbrand tells the amazing story of Second Lieutenant Louis Zamperini, a crew member aboard the B-24 bomber "The Green Hornet."[2] In 1942, he and ten other men were flying a search and rescue mission over the Pacific. That specific aircraft (nicknamed "the lemon plane" because of its ongoing mechanical difficulties) crashed into the ocean some 850 miles off the coast of Oahu. Eight of the eleven crew members died, leaving only Zamperini, Russell Allen Phillips, and Francis McNamara afloat on their life raft. With little food, no water, and the constant threat of shark attacks, storms, and occasional gunfire from Japanese planes, the three men struggled for their lives. McNamara died after thirty-three days; miraculously, Phillips and Zamperini made it to the Marshall Islands after an incredible forty-seven days at sea.

Zamperini was initially listed as missing, then declared dead a year and a day after his disappearance. But he'd been captured by the Japanese navy and spent three years in prison camps until he was freed at the end of the war in 1945. He enjoyed a hero's return home but encountered great difficulty in the transition to normal life, struggling with post-traumatic stress disorder, alcoholism, and a strained marriage. With his wife's encouragement, Zamperini attended the 1949 Billy Graham Crusade in Los Angeles where he put his faith in Christ. For the first time, he discovered the meaning of true forgiveness. Remarkably, in 1950, he returned to Japan to forgive some of the prison guards who abused him.

Coming Home

You may not have had a journey away from home like Zamperini, but many of us have left home—if not physically, then emotionally. If that's you, what took you away? Success at work? Fame and fortune? A new way of life? Often those journeys are the selfish pursuit of some desire or longing. When we try to return home we have no life to breathe into others. The parable of the prodigal son in Luke 15:11–32 is a good example of a man setting out on a journey in search of selfish gain and desire. In Luke 15:13–18 we read:

> Not long after that, the younger son got together all he had, set off for a distant country and there squandered his wealth in wild living. After he had spent everything, there was a severe famine in that whole country, and he began to be in need. So he went and hired himself out to a citizen of that country, who sent him to his fields to feed pigs. He longed to fill his stomach with the pods that the pigs were eating, but no

one gave him anything. When he came to his senses, he said, "How many of my father's hired men have food to spare, and here I am starving to death! I will set out and go back to my father and say to him: 'Father, I have sinned against heaven and against you.'"

Whatever the reason and regardless of how far you've gone, it's time to return home. Repent and embrace the forgiveness Christ offers so you can be the hero who brings life to your family, friends, and community. You may feel that's impossible—that you've been gone too long or journeyed too far—but the beautiful and redeeming news of Jesus Christ is that God the Father eagerly awaits your return.

Life Giving Gifts

What gift of life can we offer when we return? Terence Real answers that when he talks about "relational heroism."[3] It's the idea we don't have to win a war on the battlefield or achieve greatness on the athletic field. We can be everyday heroes in our relationships.

One of the primary ways we do that is to understand how we've been uniquely gifted by God and how those gifts give life to others. *All* of us have them. If we don't know what they are we can think of qualities

> **You may not** *have had a* **journey away from home** *like Zamperini* **but many of us have left home—***if not physically, then* **emotionally.** *If that's you,* **what took you away?**

our best male friends say we have. Thoughts like these will emerge: "I'm an encourager . . . I'm compassionate . . . I'm fun to be around . . . I know how to bring out the best in people."

If we know our gifts but don't want to broadcast them because that's bragging, remember God intends them for *others*, so technically, they're not ours. The people in our life need them so they can move in directions they are fearful of or do things they think are impossible. By offering them those gifts we offer ourselves up for their good. Jesus reminds us of this when He says:

> My command is this: Love each other as I have loved you. Greater love has no one than this, that he lay down his life for his friends. You are my friends if you do what I command. I no longer call you servants, because a servant does not know his master's business. Instead, I have called you friends, for everything that I learned from my Father I have made known to you. You did not choose me, but I chose you and appointed you to go and bear fruit—fruit that will last. Then the Father will give you whatever you ask in my name. This is my command: Love each other. (John 15:12–17)

We don't have to **win a war on the battlefield** *or achieve* **greatness on the athletic field.** *We can be* **everyday heroes** *in our* **relationships.**

We're commanded to lay down our lives for others. How can we start? For some of us it means being emotionally available for our wives. Others need to leave work at the office and be present and engaged with our children. Still others can mentor or coach to call out that God-created strength in an athlete or student.

As you discover the life-giving qualities God has given you, use them boldly. You'll experience the incredible potential you have for a hero's welcome and will never be the same. Neither will the people you love—and God will be overjoyed with His son who's finally come home.

Challenge

Make a list of your life-giving qualities—and don't hesitate to ask the people who know you to help. Look for an opportunity to share one of them with someone this week. Continue doing that with the other qualities until sharing them becomes a lifelong habit.

Action
Out of Reflection

*Action springs not from thought,
but from a readiness for responsibility.*[1]
Dietrich Bonhoeffer

In chapter ten, I mentioned one of my seminary professors, Dr. Ray Anderson. I was fortunate enough to develop a wonderful friendship with Ray and appreciated many things about him. One of them was his love for pastor and theologian Dietrich Bonhoeffer, a Lutheran in Nazi Germany who was martyred for his faith.

Ray loved Bonhoeffer's theological praxis, which refers to how we combine reflection and action. Bonhoeffer didn't just think deeply about the theology he read and taught. He allowed it to spur him to engagement with the world around him. In 1933, while serving a two-year appointment as pastor of two German-speaking Protestant churches in London, he received a letter from theologian Karl Barth challenging him to return to Berlin "on the next ship" because "the house of your church is on fire."[2] How, Barth wondered, could Bonhoeffer leave Germany while the Nazis lulled the church into compliance with their agenda? Two years later, Bonhoeffer returned to direct the underground seminary for the Confessing Church at Finkenwalde.

In 1939, Bonhoeffer left for New York at the invitation of Union Theological Seminary. But after much inner struggle, he wrote this to Reinhold Niebuhr, a theologian and professor at Union:

> I have come to the conclusion that I made a mistake in coming to America. I must live through this difficult period in our national history with the people of Germany. I will have no right to participate in the reconstruction of Christian life in Germany after the war if I do not share the trials of this time with my people. . . . Christians in Germany will have to face the terrible alternative of either willing the defeat of their nation in order that Christian civilization may survive or willing the victory of their nation and thereby destroying civilization. I know which of these alternatives I must choose but I cannot make that choice from security."[3]

True to his word, he returned to Germany to engage in the struggle for the life of the church and its people. The time between Barth's letter and his ultimate return shows he struggled to make the right decision. But I admire him for wrestling through it and committing to a course of action. Like Bonhoeffer, we sometimes struggle to do the right thing. Hopefully, as we strive to be men of God, we will be men of great and timely action.

In 1937, in the midst of his struggle, Bonhoeffer wrote *The Cost of Discipleship* (based on Jesus' teaching on the Sermon on the Mount).[4] When I read it, I was struck as much by Jesus' movement from contemplation to action as by His specific teaching. The passage begins with Jesus withdrawing to reflect and teach. "Now when he saw the crowds, he went up on a mountainside and sat down. His disciples came to him, and he began to teach them" (Matt. 5:1–2). When it ends, He comes down from the mountain and actively engages the world. "When he came down from the mountainside, large crowds followed him. A man with leprosy came and knelt before him and said, 'Lord, if you are willing, you can make me clean.' Jesus reached out his hand and touched the man. 'I am willing,' he said. 'Be clean!' Immediately he was cured of his leprosy" (Matt. 8:1–3). The Sermon on the

> *Hopefully,* **as we strive to be men of God,** *we will be* **men of great** *and* **timely action.**

Mount and the life of Dietrich Bonhoeffer are great lessons on the balance between what Richard Rohr calls retreating and confronting—in other words, the balance between reflection and action.[5]

Finding the Balance

Action without thought usually comes from a very reactionary place, tapping into the worst of us. It's our impulsive side rearing its ugly head, and we usually fail at giving life, courage, and confidence to those we love. For instance, if our wives complain we're not doing enough to help them, we can act aggressively with frustration or passively with dutiful response. Either way, we provide a few weeks of temporary relief before things go back to the way they were; or we do things that don't really connect with her needs.

But that short-circuits our need for deep reflection on *why* she says we're not doing enough. We need to listen thoughtfully, then take responsibility for thinking and acting differently. As mentioned earlier in the book, it's not enough that we work to provide a good living, attend kids' games, and sit in a pew at church. We must emotionally engage with the people we love.

That can happen. We *can* do things differently. We need to retreat and reflect as Jesus often did: "One of those days Jesus went out to a mountainside to pray, and spent the night praying to God" (Luke 6:12; see Mark 1:35, 6:45–46, 14:32–34; Luke 4:42 and 5:16 for other examples). Then we need to take what we've learned and confront the world with courage and confidence.

Challenge

What can you specifically do today to begin the process of reflection?
Once you've done that, how can you put what you've learned into action?

Vocation

Hearing God's Call

Many people mistake our work for our vocation. Our vocation is the love of Jesus.[1]
Mother Teresa

When I was in high school my grandfather was approaching sixty-five, and I thought for sure he was looking forward to retirement. One day, I asked him when he planned to make it official and enjoy the good life.

He looked at me like I was crazy. "I'm never going to retire," he said. "What would I do—sit in my rocking chair on the porch and die?" As we talked, he shared wisdom with me about work and vocation I have never forgotten. He explained it's a blessing—part of God's created order for our lives—and we are fortunate to work. He was confident God created him to care for and work at the things He brought his way. He also found meaning in reflecting God's character through what he'd done each day.

That's a concept of work that goes back to Genesis one. God worked and cared for His creation as He created life out of darkness. He made man (Hebrew "adam") in His image, forming him from the ground (Hebrew "adamah") and naming him Adam (an act of sovereign care). Then He commanded him to work and care for the land from which he'd been taken (Gen. 2:15) and to care for His creatures by naming them (Gen. 2:19). [2] In the words used and the commands given, we see a deep connection between our identity as men and our responsibility to imitate God in working and caring.

But didn't God tell Adam the ground would be cursed and not produce like it used to (Gen. 3:17–19)? Doesn't that mean work is a curse? I have heard some men argue this. But note that, in the midst of the curse, God enabled Adam to live out his created image. In Genesis 3:20 he demonstrates his responsibility to care for Eve by naming her—and in 3:23, though banished from the garden, he's back at work caring for the land.

Work is *a blessing—part of* **God's created order for our lives—** *and we are* **fortunate to work.**

Still, because we're fallen and sinful, work can be hard. Sometimes it's because we're lured into jobs by materialism and success; at other times, because we just fall into something that allows us to pay bills, send kids to college, and provide food and clothing. Either way, it's drudgery (versus something that allows us to fully engage our God-given image as men). That disconnect can be so profound we often organize our lives around escaping it. Seth Godin writes, "Instead of wondering when your next vacation is, maybe you should set up a life you don't need to escape from."[3]

To do that, it's worth noting the word "vocation" comes from the Latin word *vocatio,* meaning "summons."[4] In other words, our vocation is a summons calling out to us. That means listening to the same person who said to Jesus, "This is my Son, whom I love; with him I am well pleased," telling Him His work would flow from the unbreakable tie they had as Father and Son (Matt. 3:17; see chapter seven also). In the same way, God says to us, "You are my son, whom I love; with you I am well pleased." That enables us to relax in our rock-solid identity as His son, understand the gifting and talents He's given us, and pursue a career with the confidence He'll guide us to the work He has for us.

> **Vocation is** *a summons* **calling out to us.** *That means* **listening to the same person who said** *to Jesus,* **"This is my Son,** *whom* **I love; with him I am well pleased."**

No matter what kind of work you're in, my hope is you arrived there by hearing His call to you as a son and His leading for you as a disciple. If so, you've found vocation. If not, I hope you'll begin the journey of discovery by listening to His voice. What is He saying to you? What has He created you to do? Let your vocation flow out of your relationship with the Father, rather than the other way around.

Challenge

Set aside ten minutes each day this week to listen to what God is telling you about your vocation. Do you enjoy your work? If so, thank Him for it. Is it drudgery? If so, is it possible He's calling you to something new? Talk to a friend or vocational counselor about the stirrings you feel.

Conclusion

That's all there is, there isn't any more.[1]
From the children's book *Madeline*

"That's all there is, there isn't any more" is from the closing page of *Madeline*, one of my favorite books as a child and one my daughter loves me to read to her. It's the perfect children's story with a nice, tidy ending that allows the reader to move on to something else.

My fear is many of us will view this book the same way—that in a quest to put in the quick fix, we'll have just *read* it and move on because our story is done. But our story as men is *never* done. There is always more. The concepts we've covered and the study guide you're about to use aren't a one-time task to complete. They're the mile markers for a lifestyle, an exciting adventure in everyday, intentional living that requires an ongoing engagement with God, others, and ourselves.

The key to staying on course is continually listening to God's call. *That* relationship is the key to becoming the man God desires us to be and others need us to be. As our friendship with Him grows, we'll have the courage to face ourselves and do what's required to be life-givers to those we love. That's when we'll have the joy of knowing our story is one God writes with a powerful hand on the pages of eternity.

A final note: Though this book is written with and for Christian men, every man—Christian or non-Christian, young or old—struggles on the masculine journey. Share these ideas with non-Christian men and pray they'll be drawn to the Father who loves them and the Savior who died for them. After all . . . that's the greatest masculine journey there is.

Small Group Guide

Participation in men's small groups is one of the key ways I have been challenged, affirmed, and transformed over the years. The interaction is great; the encouragement and support is strong; and the life change is significant. My hope is this guide will give you and the guys in your group the same experience. If this is your first time leading a group, be encouraged. You don't need to be an expert and have a lot of experience. All you need is a willing and prayerful heart.

I've compiled sixteen weeks of material, and there are a couple of ways to use it. You can read one chapter per week and discuss it. Or you can read the entire book and then begin the study. It's up to you. I encourage you to meet weekly because that encourages momentum and strengthens your resolve to an ongoing commitment. If you can't or choose not to, make a schedule of meetings so the group can plan for and commit to the process.

Each study contains the following elements: the *objective*, which is what I hope you'll accomplish (Feel free to come up with your own, too.); *reflection questions,* so you can discuss what you've learned; a follow-up *exercise;* and a *prayer.*

Week fifteen helps the group start its wrap-up by providing time for reflection. Week sixteen ties things together with what I call *action*. I recommend you look at it before the group starts and brainstorm ideas for it during the early weeks. I've found the anticipation of a closing action helps everyone own it when the time comes.

Also, feel free to adapt and contextualize this structure to meet the needs of your group. I've intentionally left out some things so as to not be too directive. For example, I didn't include an opening prayer; and while there are a few extra verses provided, the chapters already have the key ones, so I'm counting on you to refer there when needed.

Week One

Jumping In and Getting to Know Each Other

Objective

To begin building a bond with each other by establishing ground rules, sharing basic information about who we are, and sharing goals

Ground Rules

Here are a few I use with my clients. Add others if you feel it will help (for instance, you might want to have an attendance policy.)

1. Be curious. When we are curious, we are in a posture of open-ness. We are listening rather than judging.[1]
2. Whatever is shared in the room, stays in the room.[2] This is extremely important. Otherwise, the group won't open up and be vulnerable.
3. Don't talk over others. Respect each man's right to share.

Introductions

Each man should introduce himself and share these things: a brief bio (family, work, hobbies, etc.); why he's in the group (or what he hopes to get out of it); and what he pictures happening to indicate real change is occurring. (The last question may seem a bit general but I find men who picture what they want to see happen—or what change looks like—are more likely to stay motivated as they see it taking place.)

Closing

Discuss helpful information such as the schedule of meetings and how to prepare for next week.

Prayer

Week Two *(Chapter One)*

Archetypes: The Making of Men

Objective

To increase our awareness of male archetypes that shape and influence us

Reflection Questions

1. What do you think of the four male archetypes the chapter covers (king, warrior, sage, and lover)?
2. Which one do you spend the most time trying to emulate? How successful are you at not giving in to its shadowy side? Are there any lessons you've learned about resisting it you can share?
3. In the community where you spend most of your time, which archetype gets the most attention? How does its shadowy side show itself?
4. Aside from David, is there another Bible character whose version of masculinity you identify with? Why?

Exercise

Draw four columns on a piece of paper. Label them "king," "warrior," "sage," and "lover." In each column, write several characteristics of each that you embody. Also, write down several shadowy sides you struggle with.

This will help you see how you express your masculinity. As you go through the study, refer to the columns so you can see how your masculinity is changing. Make a habit of asking, "What characteristics do I want to keep? Which ones do I need to change?"

Prayer

Week Three *(Chapter Two)*

Extremes: A Tale of Two Men

Objective

To assess how balanced you are between passivity and aggressiveness

Reflection Questions

1. Do you struggle with being too passive or too aggressive? How does that express itself?
2. Think about the men who have played a major role in your life. Are they too passive or too aggressive? How has their influence affected you?
3. How can you take the positive in what they taught you and separate it from the negative?
4. What lessons can we learn from Jesus about the balance between passivity and aggressiveness? See John 2:13–17 (aggressive) and John 8:1–11 (passive).

Exercise

Sometime this week ask someone you trust which characteristic you live out most frequently, including examples. Ask their advice on how to be more balanced.

It's a risky question for two reasons. One, you're putting the other person on the spot and they may not feel comfortable answering it. (You can hedge that by telling them they can have time to think about it.) Two, you could become defensive or angry—and even withdraw if you don't like the answer. But the risk is worth the reward. It will give you a great opportunity to discover who you are and the changes you need to make. And more than likely, it will *strengthen* your relationship with that person because they loved you enough to speak the truth—and you had the courage to hear it and do something about it (Proverbs 9:8).

Prayer

Week Four *(Chapter Three)*
Fathering: Breathing Life into the Son

Objective
To understand the role your father or other men in your life had in giving you life or creating hunger for a relationship that didn't exist

Reflection Questions
1. Now that you've read the chapter, describe what it means for your father or other male figure to be a life-giver.
2. Have you experienced that? If so, tell the group what it was like (including things you appreciated and learned).
3. If you didn't, what wounds or hunger have you been left with? What insights can the other guys offer about how to handle it?

Exercise
Identify a man in your community who needs a good male mentor (he can be of any age). Ask Jesus if you are the person who can provide that. If you are, what steps can you take to start the relationship?

On the other hand, if you need a mentor, identify someone who could fulfill that role. Pray for guidance about whether to contact him. The Lord will be faithful in showing you what to do ("Commit to the Lord whatever you do, and your plans will succeed." Proverbs 16:3; and "In his heart a man plans his course, but the Lord determines his steps." Proverbs 16:9)

Prayer

Week Five *(Chapter Four)*

Depression: Trapped in Our Anger

Objective

To figure out if you struggle with depression but hide it with things like anger, work, drinking, drugs, pornography, and/or sexual relationships

Reflection Questions

1. What were some of the messages you heard growing up about what it means to be a man? Who did those messages come from? Were they accurate?
2. What were you taught about expressing your feelings and emotions? Did you ever see your father or other significant male express emotions and feelings in a healthy way?
3. Did he struggle with depression? Did he mask it with anger, workaholism, pornography, drinking, or other things? Have you picked up on any of those habits? What do you need to do to get rid of them?
4. If you are struggling with depression, how might God use it to draw you closer to Him?

Exercise

Pay attention this week to how you handle feelings. Do you express them in a healthy way or stuff them and cope with an unhealthy habit? For example, if you feel unloved but can't express it, do you withdraw from others and use alcohol or pornography? Also, if you think you're depressed, ask for help. If you think someone else in the group is depressed, reach out and walk through it with him.

Prayer

Week Six *(Chapter Five)*
Silence: The Relational Abyss

Objective
To honestly assess how you communicate with the important people in your life

Reflection Questions
1. Would you describe yourself as expressive or non-expressive? What experiences and influences have made you that way?
2. What fears do you have in communicating with others? What drives those fears?
3. Are you aware that when you fail to communicate with your wife you force her to "fill the void"? How does that usually work out?
4. What's an example of positive, open communication you've had with someone? What made it that way? How did you feel during and after the conversation?

Exercise
Think of one person in your life who needs you to communicate with them and what they need to hear. Why are you holding back? Take the risk this week to talk with them.

Prayer

Week Seven *(Chapter Six)*
Stuck: Moving Out of Your Box

Objective
To understand if you're stuck inside your boundaries of competence

Reflection Questions
1. Larry Crabb describes men as living within the "boundaries of their competence." Which boundaries do you live within?
2. What happens within those boundaries that affirms you and gives you meaning?
3. Are you a "fix it" guy? What happens when you can't fix it? How does that make you feel? What do you do when you feel that way?
4. What's it like when you move beyond your boundaries of competence and communicate or handle issues with others? Do you feel adequate or inadequate? Do you have the tools you need to do that well? If not, what steps can you take to get them?

Exercise
Choose a relationship outside your boundary and intentionally engage with that person. For example, if you struggle to communicate with your wife or girlfriend, talk with her. Ask open ended questions that allow her to share her feelings. An example is, "How does that make you feel?" or "What went through your mind when she said that?"

If you struggle spending time with your teenage son, spend time with him. If you're not sure which setting is best, ask which works for him. Let go of trying to have all the answers and fix everything. Be patient, present, listen, and engage—even if things get messy.

Prayer

Week Eight *(Chapter Seven)*
Encounter: Shaped by the Other

Objective
To understand, accept, and enjoy our status as sons loved by our heavenly Father; and gain insight on how our earthly fathers did or didn't support that

Reflection Questions
1. How does this chapter define "identity"?
2. Where do you find your identity—in your relationship with God our Father or having to achieve and do things for Him? Why?
3. What implications does Jesus' baptism and affirmation as His Father's beloved Son have on your relationship with the Father? Are you confident He unconditionally loves and accepts you? Why or why not? How has that affected your relationship with Him?
4. Do you feel unconditionally loved and accepted by your *earthly* father? Why or why not? How has that affected your relationship with him?

Exercise
Make a list of the things you build your identity on. Are they rooted in the unconditional love and acceptance of the Father or other things?

If you've built it on something other than His love, take this step to let go of it. For one month, set aside five minutes every morning and evening for prayer and quiet so you can sense God's affirmation that He unconditionally loves and accepts you. Use Psalm 103, Isaiah 30:18, 49:14–16, and Romans 8:31–39 to guide your reflection on that great truth. Also, ask Him to instruct you about how to center your identity on Him.

Prayer

Week Nine *(Chapter Eight)*
Vulnerability: Opening Ourselves Up

Objective
To begin experiencing the health, excitement, and vitality of vulnerable relationships

Reflection Questions
1. When you think of being vulnerable what comes to mind? What scares you about that?
2. In what ways was Jesus Christ vulnerable in His life and relationships?
3. How is vulnerability a double-edged sword?
4. How would you lose power if you became more vulnerable? Do you think it's worth the risk?

Exercise
Identify one person in your life who would benefit from your increased vulnerability. Do you get excited or fearful thinking about what may happen? What are specific, tangible things you can do to be more vulnerable with that person? Put at least one of them into practice this week.

Prayer

Week Ten *(Chapter Nine)*
Intimacy: Being Known

Objective
To start the process of experiencing deeper intimacy in your relationships

Reflection Questions
1. How would you define nonsexual intimacy?
2. What are some of the challenges you face in your attempts at intimacy?
3. Is your intimacy level with others what you want it to be? Why or why not?
4. Describe your intimacy with God. How can you experience it on a deeper level?
5. Do you project an image that keeps you from intimacy with other people? If so, what is it? What keeps you from being more authentic? What can you do to overcome that?

Exercise
Spend extra time this week praying God will show you what an intimate relationship with Him looks like. One of the first steps is to be honest—which requires being vulnerable with Him. Then you can prayerfully seek ways in which your intimacy with Him leads to intimacy with other people.

Prayer

Week Eleven *(Chapter Ten)*

Receiving: Taking Care of Ourselves

Objective

To accept the truth that self-care isn't an act of selfishness; it's an investment in those you care about

Reflection Questions

1. Describe how self-care benefits you *and* the people you know.
2. Who are the people who would benefit most from your self-care? Why?
3. Of the four areas of self-care (mental, physical, spiritual, and relational) which are you most successful at and which do you struggle with the most? Why?
4. Do you take a Sabbath each week? Why or why not? How could it benefit you?

Exercise

Draw four columns on a piece of paper. In each one, write an area of self-care. Write down one thing you can do in each area to make it a more regular part of your life. Don't overanalyze; just put down what naturally comes to mind.

Over the next few months, put those ideas into practice. You don't have to do each one every day; the key is to find a healthy rhythm that works for you. As each becomes a habit, add a new one in that area—and watch your skill at self-care grow!

Prayer

Week Twelve *(Chapter Eleven)*

Giving: Returning Home to Community

Objective

To learn how to be a life-giving man in your community and relationships

Reflection Questions

1. Have you been away from home physically or emotionally? For how long? Why?
2. What were you hoping to find? Did you? What did you learn while you were away?
3. Do you feel at home with God or are you on the run from Him?
4. God loves you, PERIOD. Do you believe that? Why or why not? Can you let Him love you or are you punishing yourself for something you've done?

Exercise

Write down some of the gifts God has uniquely given you. If you have a hard time coming up with something, ask a friend or one of the men in the group to help. Identify one person you can share your gifts with this week.

Prayer

Week Thirteen *(Chapter Twelve)*
Action: Out of Reflection

Objective
To practice the balance between reflection and action

Reflection Questions
1. When facing a decision or issue, do you spend most of your time reflecting or acting? Which of the two should you do more?
2. What hinders you from thoughtfully reflecting? What hinders you from taking action?
3. What role does passivity play in your movement from reflection to action? What role does aggressiveness play?
4. Can you identify an experience where you struck a balance between reflection and action? What enabled you to do that? What was that experience like?

Exercise
Identify an issue in your life that needs to be resolved. Set aside time for reflection (prayer, silence, and Sabbath) and then move into action (problem solving and participating). If it needs to be resolved in a few days, reflect for a few hours before taking action. If you have a month, try a few weeks of reflection. In either case, let your action be guided by your reflection.

Prayer

Week Fourteen *(Chapter Thirteen)*
Vocation: Hearing God's Call

Objective
To discover the freedom of connecting our work to our identity in God

Reflection Questions
1. What was the meaning of work communicated to you as you grew up? How does that influence the way you view work today?
2. Does your work flow out of your identity in God or does your identity come from your work? How does each affect you?
3. What kind of work has God called you to? Have you listened or ignored Him? Is there anything that scares you about listening?

Exercise
Think about your childhood for a moment. Write down the things you dreamed about doing for work. Where did those ideas come from? God? Your parents? Friends? Teachers? Coaches? How closely connected are those dreams to your work today? Are you disappointed or discouraged by that?

What needs to happen for you to do the work you really want to do? Could God be calling you to that? What steps can you take to find out if that's His will?

Prayer

Week Fifteen
Closing Reflection

Objective
To give the group time to think about the last fourteen weeks together

Reflection Questions
1. What was the first thing that changed in your life and relationships when you read the book and started this study?
2. In what areas have you grown the most in the last fourteen weeks?
3. What concepts have you most struggled with? What will help you move past those struggles and achieve success?

Exercise
Take time to encourage and breathe life into each other. For instance, acknowledge another guy's strengths, thank someone for their support, tell another man he's a good role model and that you want to be like him, or affirm someone as a good dad and husband.

Prayer

Week Sixteen
Closing Action

Objective
To give the group a chance to act on its last fifteen weeks of reflection

Reflection Questions
1. What do you most appreciate about your experience with the group? What are the most important lessons you've learned?
2. What things can the group keep on its prayer list for you?

Exercise
Over the last fifteen weeks, we've individually reflected on our life and relationships. We've also tried new ways of giving life to others. Now it's time to think about a life-giving action we can do as a group. Here are some ideas—but feel free to brainstorm others, too.

Ideas
A mission trip
A service project
A retreat or camping trip
A father/son trip or event (you can bring your sons, dads, grand-dads, uncles, cousins, or other significant men in your life)

Prayer

Notes

Introduction

1. Lee Thomas, *The Billy Sunday Story* (Murfreesboro, TN: Sword of the Lord Publishers, 2005), 282.

2. Jeffrey Kluger and James Lovell, *Apollo 13* (New York: Mariner Books, 2006), 69.

3. "The Free Dictionary," *http://www.thefreedictionary.com/cairn*.

Chapter One: Archetypes—The Making of Men

1. Alfred Tennyson, *In Memoriam A. H. H.* (Mansfield, NY: Blanche McManus, 1900), 127.

2. "Dictionary.com," *http://dictionary.reference.com/browse/archetype*.

3. "Archetype," *http://en.wikipedia.org/wiki/Archetype*.

4. For examples, see Robert Moore and Douglas Gillette, *King, Warrior, Magician, Lover: Rediscovering the Archetypes of the Mature Masculine* (San Francisco: Harper, 1991); Jon Eldredge, *Wild at Heart (Revised and Updated): Discovering the Secret of a Man's Soul* (Nashville: Thomas Nelson, 2011) who identifies them as lover, warrior, sage, king; R. Rohr and J. Martos, *The Wild Man's Journey: Reflections on Male Spirituality* (Cincinnati: St. Anthony Messenger Press, 1996) who pick up on Moore and Gillette's archetypes and talk at length about the positive and negative qualities of each; and Stu Weber, *Four Pillars of a Man's Heart: Bringing Strength into Balance* (Sisters, OR: Multnomah Publishers, 1999) who uses king, warrior, mentor, and friend.

Chapter Two: Extremes—A Tale of Two Men

1. Friedrich Von Schlegel, *Idea 74 in Selected Ideas (1799–1800)*, and *Roman Structure: Dialogue on Poetry and Literary Aphorisms*, transl. Ernst Behler (Pennsylvania University Press, 1968).

2. "WFFA.com," *http://www.wfaa.com/news/local/fight-club-concerns-parents-and-police-92274479.html* (April 27, 2010).

Chapter Three: Fathering—Breathing Life into the Son

1. C. S. Lewis, *Reflections on the Psalms* (Orlando: Harcourt Books, 1958), 110.

2. Richard Rohr and Joseph Martos, *The Wild Man's Journey: Reflections on Male Spirituality* (Cincinnati: St. Anthony Messenger Press, 1996), 93–94.

3. Larry Crabb, Don Michael Hudson, and Al Andrews, *The Silence of Adam: Becoming Men of Courage in a World of Chaos* (Grand Rapids: Zondervan, 1995), 147.

Chapter Four: Depression—Trapped in Our Anger

1. Archibald Hart, *Unmasking Male Depression: Recognizing the Root Cause to Many Problems Such as Anger, Resentment, Abusiveness, Silence, Addictions, and Sexual Compulsiveness* (Nashville: Thomas Nelson, 2001), 8.

2. *Goodwill Hunting* (Miramax Films, 1997).

3. Parker Palmer, *Let Your Life Speak: Listening for the Voice of Vocation* (San Francisco: Jossey-Bass, 1999).

4. Hart, *Unmasking Male Depression*.

5. Terence Real, *I Don't Want to Talk About It* (New York: Scribner, 2003).

6. Ibid., 23–24.

7. Ibid., 22.

8. Palmer, *Let Your Life Speak*, 57–58.

9. Ibid., 58.

Chapter Five: Silence—The Relational Abyss

1. *Cool Hand Luke* (Jalem Productions, Warner Brothers/Seven Arts, 1967).

2. Larry Crabb, Don Michael Hudson, and Al Andrews, *The Silence of Adam: Becoming Men of Courage in a World of Chaos* (Grand Rapids: Zondervan, 1995), 89ff.

3. Ibid., 98.

4. Terence Real, *I Don't Want to Talk About It: Overcoming the Secret Legacy of Male Depression* (New York: Scribner, 2003), 146.

Chapter Six: Stuck—Moving Out of Your Box

1. Jason Love, *http://www.quotegarden.com/men.html*.
2. Larry Crabb, Don Michael Hudson, and Al Andrews, *The Silence of Adam: Becoming Men of Courage in a World of Chaos* (Grand Rapids: Zondervan, 1995), 53.
3. Ibid., 54.

Chapter Seven: Encounter—Shaped by the Other

1. Kenneth Paul Kramer, *Martin Buber's I and Thou: Practicing Living Dialogue* (Mahwah, NJ: Paulist Press, 2003), 21.
2. Richard Rohr and Joseph Martos, *The Wild Man's Journey: Reflections on Male Spirituality* (Cincinnati: St. Anthony Messenger Press, 1996), 92.
3. Henri Nouwen, *Life of the Beloved: Spiritual Living in a Secular World* (New York: The Crossroad Publishing Company, 2002), 33.

Chapter Eight: Vulnerability—Opening Ourselves Up

1. C. S. Lewis, *The Four Loves* (Orlando: Harcourt Brace & Company, 1988), 121.
2. Brené Brown, *http://www.ted.com/talks/brene_brown_on_vulnerability.html*, 2010.
3. Matt. 26:23–25; Mark 14:17–21; Luke 22:19–34; and John 13:18.
4. Herbert Anderson, *Jacob's Shadow: Christian Perspectives on Masculinity* (Louisville: Bridge Resources, 2002), 44.

Chapter Nine: Intimacy—Being Known

1. Saint Augustine, *Confessions* (Indianapolis: Hackett Publishing, 2006), 3.
2. Terence Real, *I Don't Want to Talk About It: Overcoming the Secret Legacy of Male Depression* (New York: Scribner, 2003), 43–45.
3. Ibid.,180.
4. "Spectrum Ministries," *www.spectrumministries.com,* San Diego, CA.
5. The director was E. G. von Trutzschler, known by many as "Pastor Von."

Chapter Ten: Receiving—Taking Care of Ourselves

1. Wayne Cordeiro, *Leading on Empty: Refilling Your Tank and Renewing Your Passion* (Bloomington: Bethany House, 2010), 13.
2. Rhett Smith, *The Anxious Christian: Can God Use Your Anxiety for Good?* (Chicago: Moody, 2011), 109–130.
3. Mark Gibson, "Relax Your Life Now," *http://www.relaxyourlifenow.com/glossary*.

Chapter 11: Giving—Returning Home to Community

1. Richard Rohr and Joseph Martos, *The Wild Man's Journey: Reflections on Male Spirituality* (Cincinnati: St. Anthony Messenger Press, 1996), 60.
2. Laura Hillenbrand, *Unbroken: A World War II Story of Survival, Resilience, and Redemption* (New York: Random House, 2010).
3. Terence Real, *I Don't Want to Talk About It: Overcoming the Secret Legacy of Male Depression* (New York: Scribner, 2003), 230, 277.

Chapter Twelve: Action—Out of Reflection

1. Eric Metaxas, *Bonhoeffer: Pastor, Martyr, Prophet, Spy* (Nashville: Thomas Nelson, 2011), 321.
2. Dietrich Bonhoeffer, *Dietrich Bonhoeffer Works: Vol. 13, 1ˢᵗ Ed.* (Minneapolis: Augsburg Fortress Press, 2007), 40.
3. Metaxas, *Bonhoeffer,* 321.
4. Dietrich Bonhoeffer, *Discipleship: Dietrich Bonhoeffer Works, Volume 4* (Minneapolis: Augsburg Fortress Press, 2001).
5. Richard Rohr and Joseph Martos, *The Wild Man's Journey: Reflections on Male Spirituality* (Cincinnati: St. Anthony Messenger Press, 1996), 162.

Chapter Thirteen: Vocation—Hearing God's Calling

1. Isabella D. Bunn, compil., *444 Surprising Quotes About Jesus: A Treasury of Inspiring Thoughts and Classic Quotations* (Bloomington: Bethany House, 2006), 56.
2. F. Brown, S. R. Driver, and C. Briggs, *A Hebrew and English Lexicon of the Old Testament* (Oxford: Clarendon Press, 1976), 9.
3. Seth Godin, *Tribes: We Need You to Lead Us* (New York: Penguin Group, 2008) 102.
4. *http://www.merriam-webster.com/dictionary/vocation.*

Conclusion

1. Ludwig Bemelmans, *Madeline* (New York: The Viking Press, 1939), 46.

Study Guide

1. This is a rule Todd Sandel taught me (*www.lifegatecenter.org*) in my work with him at "The Hideaway Experience" (*www.intensives.com*). I use it in therapy with all my clients.
2. Except in cases where mandated reporting is required.

Acknowledgments

I want to first thank Moody Publishers—especially my acquisitions editor, Randall Payleitner. He has believed in me and encouraged me since we first started emailing in the summer of 2010. In times of frustration when I felt I didn't have what it takes to succeed, he's been there to let me know I do. That's just another example of why we men need to affirm each other. Thank you, Randall. I want to also extend a huge thanks to my editor, Steve Lyon. I handed him a long, wordy, mess of a manuscript and with great care and attention to detail he helped me find my voice so that the important words could begin to emerge. Thank you, Steve, for all your hard work on this book. Thanks to Natalie Mills and Rachel Rounds for working so diligently to get this book into the hands of as many people as possible. She's kept me on my toes with marketing and publicity and I'm grateful. Finally, a very sincere thank-you to the rest of the phenomenal team at Moody.

My friends have been a constant source of encouragement. Whether I'm writing or just doing life, they're life-givers to me. I relish all the late nights at restaurants and coffee shops with them— not to mention weekend trips, time together in prayer, and talking about God's work in our lives. Without them I would not be who I am today. Thank you, guys.

I'm thankful for my great family who have always supported me and believed in me. I count it a blessing to have learned so much from the men in my life—especially that a man is never manlier than when he is in a deep relationship with God. For that lesson alone, I am beyond grateful.

Finally, a word of thanks to all the men I've had the privilege of working with in ministry and counseling. Your vulnerability, courage, and willingness to allow me access to your life have been a great blessing. Thanks for the great insights you've taught me about what it means to be a man.

WHAT DOES IT MEAN TO BE A MAN?

Well, if you haven't figured it out by now, we've got another option: wear a mustache.

Cut out the mustache below (or one of your own design) and post a picture of yourself with it online to join other like-minded men in figuring out what it means to be a man.

#MANBOOK

Also available as an ebook

MoodyCollective.com